WISDOM

of

KITTENS

Art Director: Gus Yoo
Designer: Latricia Watford
Editor: Franchesca Ho Sang
Photo Researcher: Benjamin DeWalt

Metro Books
122 Fifth Avenue
New York, NY 10011

ISBN: 978-1-4351-0533-1

Printed and bound in China

3 5 7 9 10 8 6 4 2

WISDOM
of
KITTENS

Compiled by
Franchesca Ho Sang

METRO BOOKS
NEW YORK

"The superior man thinks always of virtue; the **common** man thinks of **comfort**."

–*Confucius*

"To accomplish **great things**, we must not only act, but also **dream**; not only plan, but also believe."

–Anatole France

"Expect the best, plan for the worst, and prepare to be surprised."

–Denis Waitley

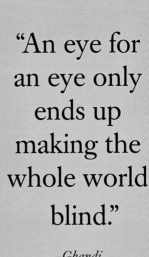

"An eye for an eye only ends up making the whole world blind."

–Ghandi

"It is a **rough road**
that **leads to** the heights of **greatness**."

–*Frank Borman*

"There is no feeling more comforting

than knowing
you are right next to
the one you love."

–Anonymous

"Stand up
to your obstacles
and do something
about them."

–Norman Vincent Peale

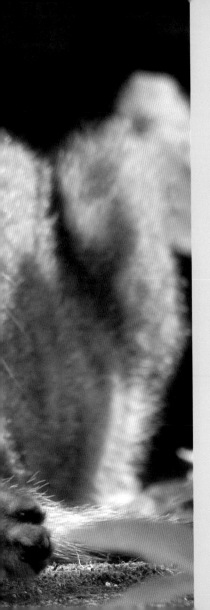

"The **best** thing to spend on your children is your **time**."

–*Louise Hart*

"'Tis the part of a **wise man** to keep himself today for tomorrow, and not venture all his eggs in one basket."

–*Miguel de Cervantes Saavedra*

"Cats are connoisseurs of comfort."

–James Herriot

"**Faith** is by which a shattered world shall **emerge** into the **light**."

–*Helen Keller*

"**Life** is a mirror and will **reflect** back to the **thinker** what he thinks into it."

–*Ernest Holmes*

"Even a cat is a lion
in her own lair."

–Indian proverb

"Life is like riding a bicycle.

To keep your balance
you must **keep moving**."

–*Albert Einstein*

"The desire for safety stands against every great and noble enterprise."

– Tacitus

"One of the greatest discoveries a man makes, one of his greatest surprises, is to find he can do what he was afraid he couldn't."

–Henry Ford

"Don't be afraid to **expand yourself,**
to **step out** of your comfort zone.
That's where the joy and **adventure lie.**"

–Herbie Hancock

"Concentration and mental toughness are the margins of victory."

-Bill Russell

"The only way to **find** the **limits** of the possible is by **going beyond** them into the impossible."

"In every
real man a
child is
hidden that
wants to **play**."

–*Friedrich Nietzsche*

"The **smallest** feline is a **masterpiece**."

–*Leonardo da Vinci*

"We must accept finite disappointment, but **never** lose infinite **hope**."

–*Martin Luther King, Jr.*

"Jump. It is not as wide as you think."

–*Joseph Campbell*

"Self-confidence is the **first** requisite to great **undertakings.**"

–*Samuel Johnson*

"It's not our differences
that divide us

it is our inability to recognize, accept, and **celebrate** those **differences**."

–*Audre Lorde*

'Live and **work** but do not forget to **play,**

to have fun in life and really **enjoy** it."

–*Eileen Caddy*

"Only those who **attempt** the absurd...
will achieve the **impossible**."

–M.C. Escher

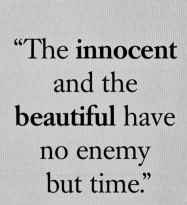

"The **innocent** and the **beautiful** have no enemy but time."

–*William Butler Yeats*

"The secret to creativity is **knowing** how to hide your **success**."

–Albert Einstein

"Love one another,
but make not a bond of love:

Let it rather be a moving sea
between shores of your souls."

–Kahlil Gibran

"**Lack** of loyalty is
one of the major causes of failure
in every walk of life."

–Napoleon Hill

"Don't be afraid
to go out
on a limb.
That's where
the fruit is."

–H. Jackson Browne

"Whatever you can do
    or dream you can begin it.
Boldness has genius,
    power and magic in it."

–*Goethe*

"**Dreams** are today's **answers** to tomorrow's questions."

–Edgar Cayce

"The whole world steps aside
for the man
who knows where he is going."

–*Anonymous*

"Who has never tasted what is bitter does not know what is sweet."

–*German proverb*

"First thoughts are the strongest."

–*Allen Ginsberg*

"Sadness is but a wall
between two gardens."

–Kahlil Gibran

"Self-assurance
is two thirds of success."

–*Proverb*

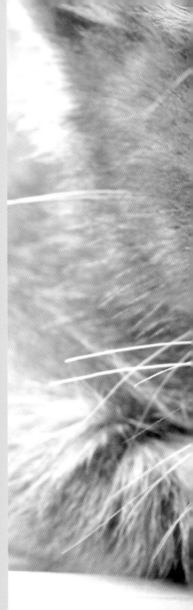

"Act as though you cannot fail but keep a humble spirit."

–Anonymous

"A friend may well be reckoned the **masterpiece** of nature."

–Ralph Waldo Emerson

"Courage doesn't always roar. Sometimes **courage is the quiet voice** at the end of the day saying. 'I will try again tomorrow.'"

–*Mary Anne Radmache*

"Friendship is the essential partnership."

–Aristotle

"Be who you are
and say what you feel,
because those who mind
don't matter, and those
who matter don't mind."

–Dr. Seuss

"Our **greatest** glory
        is not in never falling,
but rising everytime we **fall**."

–Confucius

"If you can **dream** it, you can **do it**."
‒*Walt Disney*

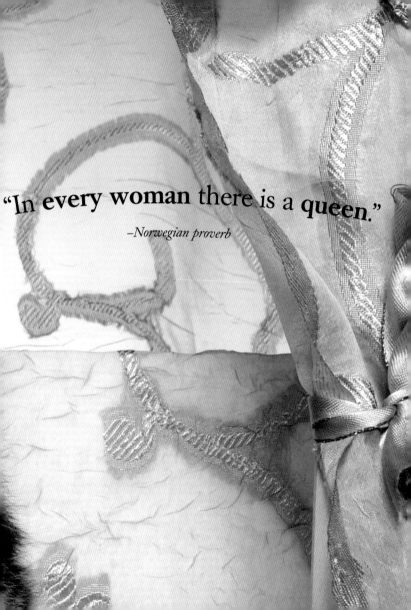

"In **every woman** there is a **queen**."

–*Norwegian proverb*

"The **future** belongs to those who prepare for it **today**."

–*Malcolm X*

"Wise men
ne'er sit and wail
their woes."

–*William Shakespeare*

"There are only two forces that **unite men**—fear and **interest**."

–Napoleon Bonaparte

"We cannot always build the future of our youth, but we can **build** our youth for the **future**."

–*Franklin D. Roosevelt*

"Some men go through a forest
and see no firewood."

–English proverb

"The price of **greatness** is responsibility."

–*Abraham Lincoln*

"Only the unknown frightens men."

–Antoine de Saint–Exupéry

"A **peaceful** man
does more than a learned one."

–*Pope John XXIII*

"Hope is the **dream** of the soul **awake**"

–French proverb

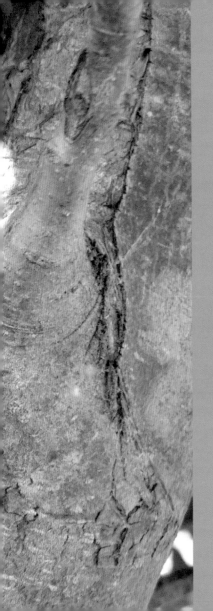

"My only advice
is to stay aware,
listen carefully
and yell for help
if you need it."

–*Judy Blume*

PICTURE CREDITS